Morley Roberts

Songs of Energy

Morley Roberts

Songs of Energy

ISBN/EAN: 9783337007256

Printed in Europe, USA, Canada, Australia, Japan

Cover: Foto ©Thomas Meinert / pixelio.de

More available books at **www.hansebooks.com**

BY

MORLEY ROBERTS.

LONDON:
LAWRENCE & BULLEN.
169, NEW BOND STREET, W.
1891

INDEX.

	PAGE
Dedication.	
The Impulse	9
Flesh and Spirit	10
The Wayfarers	11
The Worker and the Work	13
Poppy Seed	14
Miserrimus	16
The River of Pain	18
The Threads	19
The Passage Bird	21
A Lost Influence	23
For you I think, for you I weep	25
They now are few	26
Alone	28
The Child Love	29
Eros	31
True Deserts	32
Remorse and Sorrow	34
Lines	35
Inconstancy	36
A Lyrical Mood	38
If	39
Beauty	40
Ode	41
The Year's Life	44

INDEX.

	PAGE
Her Influence	45
An Unknown Dead Woman	46
The Secret	50
The Meads of Millver	53
Greece and England	56
At Delphi	57
From the Greek	62
The Dead Mistress	63
The Two Birds	69
Grotesquerie	73
Death and the Painter	82
Sonnets	85 to 97

DEDICATION.

Never know the worst of me,
 Think me always good;
Strive not to the lowest depths,
 Swim upon the flood.

Take what there is best in me,
 Love the better man,
And endure the evil, dear,
 If you dare and can.

SONGS OF ENERGY.

THE IMPULSE.

THE impulse: that's the thing;
　　To love and then to sing,
To work and dare be glad,
To dream and go half mad
With vague desire to do
Something that shall be true,
To love and bring again
Fire to the heart and brain!

Whence comes it? How or where?
I cannot yet declare,
For any man who could
Might say he understood
That thing we term our art,
But whence we subtly start
To prove ourselves must be
Left to Eternity.

FLESH AND SPIRIT.

The flesh is lord of life until
Immortal love doth all fulfil,
When spirit straightway springs afresh
Out of the very heart of flesh.

But till the body grows divine
The spirit cannot wake and shine,
And till the spirit loves the clay
'Tis only fit to cast away.

SONGS OF ENERGY.

THE WAYFARERS.

LAMENT for those who lay the dust with tears,
Weep for the sorrows of these wayfarers;
They wander on even unto the night,
    Their burden is not light.

Their eyes are dim with weeping many tears,
They have wan cheeks, alas! these wayfarers;
Their hands and hearts are weary for delight,
    For it is always night.

The crown is of grey hairs for wayfarers,
Their goblets worn cheeks full of salt, sad tears;
Their land of promise is a place named Night,
    For they have no delight.

They may not be together for their tears,
They are such solitary wayfarers;
They do not touch a friend's hand in the night,
    While waiting for the light.

They weep, such thoughts they have, these wayfarers;
Their way is but a desert of salt tears,
Wherein past woes have slain all past delight,
    And none shall spring at night.

Lament, lament ye!   Ye shall shed such tears ;
Mourn and lament!   Ye must be wayfarers.
There is a little day yet, but the night
    Shall mourn for all delight.

THE WORKER AND THE WORK.

This is the truth: that the man goes first
In the desert dead, and the best and worst
Of his critics, as even all critics must,
Like bookworms, die when the book is dust.

And this is truth: that the work he did,
Like carving done on a coffin lid,
Crumbles and fades with the features thin
That were the grave of the soul within.

And this is truth (if we think it so):
That the very suns and the seas must go,
The paintings of God, like graffiti scrawls
Done on the buried Pompeian walls.

And whether or not the soul survives
Either of God or our own sad lives,
We cannot say; but full well we know
That the best and the worst of our work must go.

POPPY SEED.

Bring forth poppy, laudanum,
   Drowsy syrups, what you will;
Lay these ghosts and make them dumb,
   Ghosts that chatter things of ill,
   Ghosts that fret but cannot kill.

Ghosts that fret but cannot kill
   (Things that will not let me sleep
By a sea that's never still,
   Where the waves for ever leap),
   Hideous things that bite and creep.

Hideous things that bite and creep
   On the shivering flesh that crawls,
Horrid hands that ever keep
   Writing jests obscene on walls
   Mixed with minatory scrawls.

Mixed with minatory scrawls,
   " Thou art weighed and wanting found,

And Belshazzar's lofty halls
   Shall be levelled to the ground
   Under which hell's worms abound ".

Where the worms of hell abound
   Is in life, thou hand of ill.
If I be a king and crowned
   Bring me poppy, what you will,
   Sleep or death, to calm or kill.

MISERRIMUS.

BE ever somewhat sad, and let not in
   The joy that, like the light, will never stay ;
     For wings she hath, and wings were made for flight.

Hug thyself closely ; keep thyself within
   The dark house, lest the advent of the day
     Should, by its glory, blind thee to the night.

For night and sorrow are the two things sure,
   And when they sudden and unlooked-for come,
     How shall thy white house hold these sombre guests ?

For they will never linger at thy door,
   Their breath shall make thy tongue, that stays them, dumb;
     For how shall doves keep eagles from their nests ?

And these are harpies. Feed them with thy soul,
   Give them thy heart, for that should satisfy,
     And gentle words with soft abated breath ;

The while within thee ask of God the dole
Of acquiescence, for with that we die ;
And quiet is the house that shelters death.

THE RIVER OF PAIN.

The sky is blue in the creek's still stream,
And the supple willows droop and dream
Where the green weed under the water grows.

Within my heart is another sky,
And other trees droop dreamily
In the distant land of the soul's repose.

The sun is bright on the grass of the spring,
And the birds are resting sweet throat and wing,
And the wind is quiet on hill and plain.

But the faint soul's herbage is not so fair,
And the birds that sang are no longer there,
For love's sweet songster is dead and slain.

So the sky grows dark to the depth of night,
And the light of the stars is no heart's light;
And the stream of life is the river of pain.

THE THREAD.

I saw them spin within the gloom
The thin, bright, twisted thread of doom.
(I see them yet within my room.)

Who drew the thread was still a child,
Rosy and slight and sweet and mild.
(She smiles not now as then she smiled.)

Who twisted up the glittering thread
Was a fair girl with golden head.
(Pale are her cheeks that once were red.)

Who cut the cord was old and white,
And as she cut her lips moved light.
She spoke a language dark as night.

She speaks in language dark as night,
The maiden fades to dark from light,
The child looks up with keen affright.

A speck of blood shines on the reel,
And blood is on the golden wheel,
And on the shears of shining steel.

The speck is but a prophecy,
The next is the fulfilment nigh,
And after —— let the living sigh.

THE PASSAGE BIRD.

He dwelt upon a barren isle,
   Whose seas and skies were cold and dim,
And never any sweet bird sang
   Its song to him.

He only heard the grating beach
   For ever lashed by that fierce gale,
Which sank the ships of which he saw
   No single sail.

His only friend was that which spoke
   No more; it died the day he came
By chance unto this hopeless land
   Which has no name.

And yet, I think, he would have been
   Less sad, although no herbage springs
For ever there, had he not heard
   At night soft wings.

They told him that he dwelt between
    Two lands of summer, and when one
Was silent, then the other woke
    To greet the sun.

But he was fixed, and could not go,
    Since hope lay sunken by the beach,
And all the ships that passed by day
    Were out of reach.

While in the night of tearless pain
    He heard the rustling wings above
Of that bright passage bird, whose name
    He knew was Love.

A LOST INFLUENCE.

A SPIRIT came (I called her Love),
   And took a woman's form that night,
Beside my fire. She seemed to me
   More than angelically bright.

Her form was slender as the stalk
   That bears the lily's crown; her face
Was like a saint's, whose purity
   Would fit some fair and heavenly place.

She did not speak. Her silence quelled
   My eager soul, that is not meek;
Until at last my heart rejoiced
   That she was still and did not speak.

For all the voices that are loud
   In exhortation would decline
To quietness, if they were met
   By silence that is half divine,

And hers was heavenly. Well I know
  She changed my very spirit's bent,
Like snow that bends a loaded branch,
  Until the hour she rose and went.

And now I am the thing I was,
  The very thing I loathe to be ;
And her salvation shall not come,
  I know for ever, back to me.

FOR YOU I THINK, FOR YOU I WEEP.

For you I think, for you I weep,
  For you I go so heavily;
For you strange ghosts disturb my sleep;
  And whisper dreadful things to me.

I cannot walk, and cannot sit;
  Fire is not warm, and for my thirst
No water runs that quenches it;
  The sun and moon are things accurst.

I may not go, and must not stay;
  I wander round, across, and through
Life's maze, grown barren day by day,
  Where once the sweetest flowers grew.

THEY NOW ARE FEW.

Let the poison-cup fall down and break,
Though I would drink, were it for your sake;
Be merciful, love, for love's at stake.

Oh, be not cold, for a wind that's chill
May blast a flower like a flame, and ill
Doth coldness come to my fervent will.

Think what you slay, if you slay me now,
A song-bird singing on summer's bough;
And singers are rare, as all avow.

There are sparrows, and hawks, and jays, and kites,
And owls for hooting at dead-o'-nights,
And a few far eagles on mountain heights.

But for the thrush, and the heavenly lark,
And the woodland spirit that sings in the dark,
And the leaf-brown linnet, how few they mark!

SONGS OF ENERGY.

So when I burn with a terrible fire,
And the bitter pangs of a strange desire,
Let love not prove you a cheat and liar.

ALONE.

OH, if it never had been for me,
   For me and the fates above,
Your eyes would never have learnt to see,
   Nor your empty heart to love.

Yet since we met, and the thing was done,
   It would be easier still
To part two streams that together run
   On the slope of a steep, high hill.

And easier far to take the rain
   From the sea when the storm is o'er,
Than to make our two hearts two again
   And our souls as they were before.

And this I know as I lie awake.
   When I know you wake to moan,
That the man you love for his own dear sake
   Is alone, for ever alone.

THE CHILD LOVE.

Come now, O woman! it is time
   To bury love, whose lips are cold
With frosts that from his grey heart climb,
   Which once was ruddy red like gold.

For if desire shall make delay
   A semblance of our first delight,
His beauteous body will decay,
   And on the morrow of this night

We two shall hate each other so
   That love will be a loathsome thing,
Whence poisoned thoughts will rise and grow
   To words that foul and mark and sting;

Until our bodies, once as fair
   And once as beautiful to see
As our dead sin that's lying there,
   My child and yours, with scars will be

As dreadful as the first harsh word
　　Which urgent bitterness begot,
That you in anguished sorrow heard
　　Yet in my kisses half forgot

And all forgave.　So lest this be
　　Take up the burden in its flowers,
And seek some hidden place where we
　　May bury this dead love of ours.

EROS.

Eros, Eros, did I see you
   With a half-extinguished torch,
Like a ghost who lights a garden
   In your shattered temple's porch?
Did I see you, hear you calling?
Answer me, whose tears are falling,
Eros, Eros, hear me calling!

Eros, Eros, did I hear you
   Clasp your hands and purple plumes,
Gleaming like a dim star fallen
   In this ghostly land of tombs?
Is the torch a sombre token
Of a life whose words are spoken,
Eros, and a heart that's broken?

TRUE DESERTS.

True deserts are not barren spots
   Of sand with nothing there:
They are fire-wasted meadows wan,
   Which once were bright and fair.

Where nothing was no heart can grieve,
   For on the long grey plain
Of empty sand no dead things mock
   The help of falling rain.

But when a garden, heavenly bright
   With promise, is disgraced
Within men's souls or on the earth,
   That is the desert waste.

And as I look I deserts see
   Within me and around,
And the fierce fire that burns us up
   In every heart is found.

Look you and quench it, lest it grow;
  And all your promise fair
Be but a mockery of the seed
  That nature planted there.

REMORSE AND SORROW.

SPEAK not of sin—your words lack force ;
    I am what fate would have me : so
Sin, and repentance, and remorse
    Are but an empty show.

And yet I'm sorry—for the dead,
    A woman poor and plain, but true,
Who loved me, so her sister said ;
    And yet—I never knew.

LINES.

Ah me, at times I do forget
All time past and all past regret,
And live. Then I remember yet
And fall and weep, till I am met
By hope's enchanted following,
And then from highest clouds I fling
My soul, and take unto the wing
Of one who soars and who may sing.
And when I seek the earth again
The grass is green. Was it the rain
Or the world's tears? Ah me, my pain
Doth, like the moon, still wax and wane.

INCONSTANCY.

She leans and clasps him. Thus the woman saith,
" I love you as my passionate life loves breath.
One lover can I have; 'tis thou or death.

" My love for thee measures my hate for death,
Yet shall he kiss my lips and suck my breath
If thou reject me." And he, answering, saith :

" What wouldst thou have ? I love, not thee, but one
Queen of a kingdom stars beyond the sun,
My soul knew her's when woman yet was none.

" If she be not, let there again be none,
Let the stars vanish with the empty sun,
And all things living perish one by one."

How idle are the words a dreamer saith,
    As idle as a shadow of the sun,
As fleeting as a frozen morning's breath ;

He who rejected her, rejected one
But took another; she who prayed for death,
Was more than glad when answer came there none.

A LYRICAL MOOD.

Away with your verses satiric
   And the saturnine muse that I wooed
I will write you a delicate lyric
   For I'm in a lyrical mood.
I will fashion a poem of phrases
   That one might imagine he wrote
Who lay among violets and daisies,
   For lovers to quote.

I have done with despair and with sighing,
   I'm a monarch commanding my muse,
And she without frowns or denying
   Will smile on her lover who woos;
She will bring me a dower of posies,
   Bouquets of poetical rhyme,
And give me her garland of roses,
   And sing all the time.

IF.

If I disdain one wish of thine,
   Tho' it may be but half expressed,
By a sweet sigh or tender sign
   Of blushing cheek or heaving breast,
May I forget what 'tis to be
Beloved by thee, beloved by thee!

And if in days to come I press
   Thy hand less warmly, half in scorn
Of our delightful tenderness,
   May I be wholly left forlorn,
And see thee, dearest, pass me by
Without a sigh, without a sigh!

BEAUTY.

Bless her! Not for her kindness; nay,
   Was she so kind after all?
What is a kiss then, say?
   'Tis but a flower on the wall,
   And she is a garden of roses and lilies full tall.

Bless her! Yes, for her beauty, given
   Up like the rose's scent
To the wind and the bending heaven,
   The stars and the firmament,
   And the universal beauty whereof her body is blent.

ODE.

Ye simple deities who haunt each spring,
Whence cooing wood-doves wing
Their way, thro' leafy avenues and mazes,
Over the meadow's daisies,
And buttercups, that match the open sun,
By pleasant streams, which run
Singing and hidden in the hollow grass,
Arching the way they pass,
I come to dream among you, and to hear
Your birds sing sweet and clear.

The linnet sings, nor leaves the fragrant hedge ;
Within the thick green sedge
The warble of the sedge-bird is so sweet
It draws my lingering feet ;
And earth-born seraph larks are chanting fair
In windless morning air,
Rising and falling with swift notes, as light
As gossamers in flight,
For filled with joy and love, they shriller sing
Even on loftier wing,

Until high heaven hears the angelic throng,
Earth's pyramid of song.

If nymphs delight these days in quiet cells,
One must be here, and dwells
By that still pool, where water-lilies fold
At even cups of gold;
If in our time no woodman hath affrighted
The dryad who delighted
In the arched hollows of yon ancient oak,
Its shadow is her cloak;
And if I hid, I might at midnight see
Some fairy company.

Here, when the mated larks look from the grass,
To see the shrew mouse pass,
When golden cups are nightly buds of green
On darkened lakes serene;
When flowers, the noontime's sun can never view,
Delight to drink the dew;
And sudden puff-balls lift some sleeping fairy,
Left by his mates more wary;
The nightingales, song wonderful, delight
The listening ear of night.

If aught I simply sing may give you pleasure,
Pour out the poet's treasure
Of beauty, as I wander down your ways,
Taught by the unseen fays;
For what you say I but repeat again
In echoing strain;
Who loves all natural loveliness, must choose
To sing, or he would lose
His dearest gift, and be a joyless man,
Despised by woodland Pan.

SONGS OF ENERGY.

THE YEAR'S LIFE.

The year is young in sorrow, and the fears
Of silver-budding spring are shed in tears.

The year grows old in sorrow; her sweet eyes
Thirst now for death before the summer dies.

The year is old in sorrow, and her wails
Float on the winds as golden autumn pales.

The year hath died in sorrow; o'er the dead
The winter snows in quiet wreaths are shed.

HER INFLUENCE.

I THINK her gentle fingers love
   A far diviner string
Than any passion which may move
   My silent heart to sing.

And when her voice grows softly sweet
   With thought my dreams have known,
The world drops down beneath my feet,
   And heaven is all my own.

For with the blessing of her face,
   The glory in her hair,
The very radiance of the place
   Shines on me unaware.

Until the music that she wakes
   From that long-silent string
Rouses my drooping soul, and makes
   Me happy as I sing.

AN UNKNOWN DEAD WOMAN.

Nay, never show me any relic left,
   This thing and this are dumb and make no sign,
Draw me no single threads from her soul's weft,
   For weft and woof through you may all be mine.

That she was this and that her portrait shows,
   Drawn by the dear dead hand that was so just;
But richer is the rich remembered rose
   Than the pot-pourri vase—half leaves, half dust.

Rather I judge the dead, that girl or this
   By the desire that burns me, for I see
That she was sweeter than her own sweet kiss,
   Than any work left to the world and me.

That this one loved her, a madonna still,
   In days divinely touched by pains that pass
And still return with joys that flood and fill
   Her soul, may better show me what she was

Than any words. That she (who dwells afar
  Half known, half guessed beyond a mist of cloud
Like a deep heaven's solitary star
  Past our clay kingdoms peopled with a crowd

Of tapers, human glow-worms, humble things
  Nor loved, nor hated) was akin to her
Bids me discern a soul that lives and sings:
  I judge her stature, yea, and can aver

This way or that she thought, and thus would think,
  If I came to her. Then again his love,
Which still is thirsty though it bends to drink
  A depth of water measured from above

By a deep star's reflection, tells me more
  Than I might learn from any praise of speech:
Ye three remake her, and your hearts' full store
  Of her delight remembered gives the reach

Of her humanity. As for her soul
  That (living as I take it unto those

Who love her) may thus live for me; its whole,
   Full, rounded, perfect, sweet, may yet disclose

Its being through the hearts that knew her face
   And all which lay behind it; saw her move
And felt her impulse; who discerned her grace
   Was the sweet gift of her completed love:

Who leant against her; who were grave of mood
   If shadows fell about her; who were gay
When the red ripple of her youthful blood
   Sang with such music as befitted day,

Unclouded from the summer dawn to eve;
   Wherefore, I knowing these (and this I dare
To bid my brain and my own soul believe),
   As far as may be now with sorrowful care

Build up what death destroyed before the time
   That set me on the path her dearest know,
And so I bring this simple gift of rhyme,
   Perhaps the first and last that I may throw

Upon her grave. If she had lived, ah me!
    I wonder: well, the world is strangely made,
I cannot grasp its order; what may be,
    With all that might have been, is past my trade

And breaks my skill. Perhaps she knows it now,
    Or, if she knows not, lies in such deep peace,
That if I looked upon her solemn brow
    I might speak words to make all troubles cease,

All troubles—yours and mine. Dear heart, farewell,
    I never knew you, and you know me not,
And yet you touch me. I discern the swell
    Of your red heart and see the simple plot

Of your sad story, which is now complete
    Within the hearts that loved you and return
Upon the paths that touched your tender feet—
    Farewell, dear heart. And yet—I yearn and yearn.

THE SECRET.

The secret that he hides
As he smiling goes,
Such a thought divides
Into joys and woes
That he scarcely knows
Anything besides.

Did you ever see
As he went along
How his lips move? He
Is shaping out a song,
Fitting, carving common words
That speak thoughts which are but clay
Into poems such as birds
Sing on every spray
In their mystic music
To the month of May.

If you be a friend
Or a gentle lover

Of an art or of a woman,
In the end
Proving that your soul is human
But so far the finer,
He, the skilled diviner,
Will admit you and discover
Strange suggestions set in song
That shall make you ache to know
Why the world is ordered wrong,
Why we vex our nature so;
And the while you wonder why,
You will wonder how the breath
Of a lyric breathing love
Sets you pondering on death.

Never think that he
Is himself aware
Of all things that be
Closely hidden there;
If you watched his wondering eyes
You might catch his glad surprise
When he found his secret came
Back to his shut lips and told
Other secrets that are hid
Underneath a pyre of flame;
Underneath a lying lid

That denies a hoard of gold.
Thus he learns, and day by day
While his woes and joys endure,
While he keeps his song-gift pure,
He will hide his soul away
In his secret songs that tell
Something, nothing, little, all,
As the hearer heareth well,
As the happy moments fall.

And meanwhile he smiles and hides,
As he pondering, doubting goes,
This his secret, which abides
Secret till the poet knows
Scarcely anything besides.

THE MEADS OF MILLVER.

"He came, soe he said, to a land wherein the people were verie friendly, but of a sadde countenance; and in this same land was a mountaine, hard to climbe and very difficult, whiche in theyre tongue was called Mylvere or Millvere, meaning the place of rest or of silence, for thither, they saide, men's souls did goe after death. And I did think it a prettie sounding word and a pleasant, and a pretty mate for silver, the which hath no fellowe in our tongue. But let the poets look to it."

IN the lonely meads of Millver,
   On the placid plateau sleeping,
   Lies a mere, whereunto sweeping
Launches out the moon of silver;
Floats a boat of carven silver,
   Like a targe that triumph wielded,
   Like a shell that Venus shielded,
On these lofty meads of Millver.

When the morning comes on Millver,
   Gently every glade discloses
   Hidden hearts, like opening roses,
Red at dawn, at eve dew silver;

But no bird breathes soft and silver
   Chimes, for all the melancho
   Of the past hours is too holy
For light melody on Millver.

But when evening comes to Millver,
   Though no lightest leaf is shaken
   Till its dew is earthward taken,
By a sprite in sudden silver
Sliding down a shaft of silver;
   Though the silence grows intenser,
   And the crowding shadows denser,
There is joy and life on Millver.

Night is day to men at Millver,
   Silence, speech that no one knoweth;
   Breath, a wind that silver bloweth
Fainter than the white moon's silver;
Silver horns with notes of silver,
   And they love to lie and hearken
   When the deep skies gloom and darken,
Or when moonbeams gleam on Millver.

Who so hath not dreamed in Millver
    Hath not known what life or death is,
    And as vain as wind his breath is;
Gold he never knew nor silver,
Not the secret moon of silver,
    Only known by those she blesses
    In the silent wildernesses
Of the undiscovered Millver.

GREECE AND ENGLAND.

GREAT is our country, but our gods are not
    The passionate beauty that made Greece divine;
We are divided, they were singly wrought
    Into one glory, like a summer vine;
We seek all ends, but they, content with one,
    Are more immortal with their Sophocles
Than we with all our empires in the sun,
    And guarded straits and close forbidden seas.

AT DELPHI.

Phœbus, at thy command I bring my vows,
And lay my offering. This I give, and this,
And this again; words and myself and blood,
Thou unstained slayer of the worser man,
Thou giver of eyesight and what subtle sense
Mocks unbelievers. I have come to thee,
Not as benignant, but to ask of fate,
That sits behind thee, even as other gods,
To take thy gifts again, to discrown brows
Unworthy, and to set me in the street
In the brave sunshine with a taste for men.
I, not ungrateful as a lesser man,
But keen to thank thee, ask the cheaper life,
Which makes rich vineyards, and the granary stored
With grain that may be eaten—I have lived
On barren hillsides in the purer air,
Difficult pastures have I toiled in; streams
That lower stayed in bounty ran by me,
And I grow weary—give me corn and oil.

I do remember, though the far faint thoughts
Of that time sink like cities on a plain

From one forth journeying, that I was not poor
In life's endowments of humanity ;
But rich as others who, as I would now,
Took from the common store their daily dues.
Phœbus, I am not strong, nor am I made
Of that fine gold which draws to hair-like wire
And beats to thicknesses which let the light,
Though gleaming on the marble of this porch
Like four square metal : I am unrefined,
Half refuse, most a dross that only seems
The purer stuff for workmanship like thine,
That most befits the road whereon I tread.
I am most weary, take away thy gifts,
Point me the place whereon this lyre shall hang
A votive offering made by one who faints,
Blind me my eyes that weary of the day :
Tell my sad tongue to sing thy songs no more
And teach my hands less subtle handicraft.

For, as I see it, there are men and men,
Some fit, some fitter for the gift of song ;
And some too weak. It is a crown that weighs
More heavy than most fetters, and a rule
Imperious as set prisons ; he who claims
The lyric sceptre hath a grave large air

Fronting the skies with equal majesty
As high Olympus. He is broadly set,
Shakes not with earthquakes, hath no dread of storms
That glorify him; rain on him is snow,
Not mist that blinds a valley; he is fair
With lucid atmosphere and long-set suns;
He claims divinity and is allowed.
When first I came to Delphi (that methinks
Is more than many years past) I was young,
Eager as a warrior, yet untried, for fight,
Rash with the youth that hath not yet discerned
Spears broken and the piercéd flesh of men,
Who deems that honour, and all honour's gifts,
Come by desire, if thirsty thoughts desire
The ample praise of unalloyed acclaim.
Now I, grown older, set myself as low
As one who claims no homage, who believes
His heritage the kingdom of the poor
Uncrowned by aspiration. Let me go.

Thou wilt not then? nay, let me plead with thee,
Thou art a god, and though a god knows men
Serenely by the sight that sees afar,
He is a greater. Being this, the less
Of our humanity is undiscerned,

As greater things by lesser. Hadst thou known
How added god-ship makes the weaker man,
As added manhood slays a god himself,
Thou hadst been merciful. Thy added gift
Has split my whole humanity; my soul
Hangs in the air, is not of heaven nor earth,
It hath no habitation, and the homes
Belovéd once are but as prisons now,
Prisons with open doors, yet strongly barred
By great conditions. Make me as thyself
Or take thy gift which breaks my bond with men.

Yet if thou wilt not, as indeed it seems
By the still air within this solemn place,
I will return and do the work, as one
Who hath no choice, who cannot be again
The parent-child that got the child-like man.
The past is past, and all my past is slain,
I stand upon the present; my desire
Being onward past the future, I must go
The path appointed—bear the appointed load,
And draw strange music from a human heart
That breaks with its divisions. Had I known
How love and song and suffering are but one,
I ne'er had come to Delphi. Yet how sweet

It is to sing, how sweet to suffer so,
How very sweet to love and grow divine
Beyond our limits. Thus indeed it is
What makes us mightier men is what no man
Hath need of—and the lesser man is he
Who is complete, and circled, duly set
Within old ordinance and stable law.
But he, the singer, prophet, seer, is one
Who breaks with other laws, the ordered peace,
And sacrifices to the one sole god
Who speaks within him.

I am more at peace,
I recognise the unalterable, and again,
Phœbus Apollo, I take my lyre whose strings
May solace óthers as I journey home.

FROM THE GREEK.

From Promachus to Phœbus! For I yield
   Curved bow and empty quiver unto thee;
   Askest thou arrows? Those dire gifts may be
Found in my foemens' hearts upon the field.

THE DEAD MISTRESS.

My heart, my dear desire, my joy, my pain,
My lover who was always like the light
To me in darkness, when the bitter rain
Of my tears ceased, when bright
In all the anguish of the bitter stars
That ruled my house, your sun
Came to me at the darkest time that scars
Such souls as mine, thinking what they have done,
Now I am dead, in very stillness bound,
I think of you still on the terrible earth,
I feel your footsteps, yea,
I stand beside you, and tho' little worth
My love goes with you in your walks to-day,
To-day, to-morrow, and shall ever go.
For now that I am dead, dearest, I know
How wrong you were when in your bitterness
And shame of loving so, you one time said.
That love that waxed must wane, till, less and less,
It vanished and was dead.

Nay, even now in the dead peace wherein
I do atone for what I thought a sin

Yet did most gladly, giving myself to you,
I know that love lives ever and is true,
Or if it be that love immortal is
Only in ceasing to adorn the frame,
That without love is worth no lover's kiss,
I thank dear death which leaves me still the same,
The same I was when I was all to you.
Have you forgiven me now because I strew
No more the blood-red passion blossoms sweet
Before your feet?
My king, my lover dear, I was not strong,
Only a poor weak woman, so the wrong
Of our vexed lives, and love,
Which of itself had almost borne me down.
So much the passion pain does dreadfully move
Our weaker bodies, made a double crown
Of earthly fire and very heavenly flame
That was too heavy. I was not your peer
In strength, or in the wisdom of the year
Not yet to be. And thus, you know, I died.

But dead although I be, my joy and pride
Is still your own; I have no child's regret
For the poor toys of a child-world's esteem.
I am content that I fulfilled your dream,
And glad that you were happier that we met.

Yea, though death took me, for you know I know
That all you said of nature was no lie,
And that you used no lover's sophistry
To blind me to the path you fain would go.
Even now in death (that once I hated so,
Thinking that it would part us) I am glad
To dream of all the bitter joy we had
When my warm heart was yours. You cannot tell
How like a warm rain fell
Your words upon the parchéd flowers of me,
That I desired to be
Bright for your hair, a chaplet for your head.
That you should deem me beautiful was strange,
Although I did believe the words you said,
For I could think that there could be no change
To make you royaller, or anything
That any woman could desire above
Your full possessing. Thus what thing could move
Your worshipped soul to mine,
Which was not great, and only grew divine
Because you loved me. Dear, I cannot mete
The mystery of it, though it was so sweet!

And though the mystery is mystery still,
Though the soul life has mazes yet untrod,
Which shall divinely open to our will

When you come with me to the throne of God.
I know that God is nature, and the voice
Which bade my body own you for its own
Was nature's self making a natural choice,
And, knowing, I have grown
To be content even with bitter death;
For did my bosom's breath
Still come and go,
As land and sea breeze blow,
Alternate in bright weather with no storm,
I still should be a child, and still be cold;
But you it was who made a woman warm
With your god's breath of fire. Though I grew old,
I never should have known how one can give
One's soul away, and find it sweet to live;
Sweeter and better yet for all the shame
That touched my white to red, and left me flame.

But now in death I have the recompense,
I know the womanhood that would have seemed
Mere words without the sympathy of sense,
The idle babble of a girl who dreamed,
Not knowing life. I had been loved indeed
(If that I doubt not, with these claspéd hands
Above my heart which knows things that escaped,
When it could beat and break, and break and bleed,

That passion makes a passion, and is shaped,
And shapes), but never loved, and all commands
Fall coldly on me till you bade me come.
And, love, I came and met you, and was dumb,
And knew myself no more,
So changed I was. The woman whence I sprang,
Like living water from the stricken stone,
Who clasped her hands and dreamed, and dreaming
    sang,
Died when you called me to the desolate shore
Whereon my lover stood, and stood alone.
She died, and I was born. Oh, pitiful
I was, dear heart, to see you so alone.
And I was glad you thought me beautiful,
And glad to know you claimed me as your own.

And now I know so well what once I saw
So dimly through my tears, that only I,
Of all earth's women, was the heart to draw
Your hand and heart together. I could die
Again, dear heart, to have that thought again,
With all its horror and its joy and pain.

But now good-night, my lover and my king,
Good-night until the morning. I must wait

A little longer here. But I could sing
With the dead lips you kissed, to know how great
My love has grown since I was his desire,
Because his work was wrought for me instead
Of the ill world that is his funeral pyre,
With the pure soul that upward burns like fire
With deathless love for the belovèd dead.

THE TWO BIRDS.

I saw two birds sit on a bough,
And bitter cold it was with frost;
The branch swayed up like the icy prow
Of a desolate bark beset and lost
In a frozen sea; I heard the sound
Of a song come over the hard black ground,
With the bitter woe of a wail from one
Who, dying, looked on the clear cold sun;
And the sounds were wailing and melody,
The joy of life that was scarce begun,
And woe for the pain that was yet to be,
Before all pain and woe were done.

A robin sat on the lower bough,
Like the scarlet of the hip,
Like a ruddy wreath on a Christmas ship,
With frost beneath on the heaving prow:
And the song he sang was of delight,
Gay and sweet, and free and wild,
Like songs that the birds sing to the night,
"Farewell. Oh, come, sweet morning child!

And drop your crumbs with a ruddy hand
On the dim white paths of the snowy land."
And he swayed with his singing to and fro,
Disdaining wind and frost and snow,
Snow winds and frost winds, howe'er they might blow;
For his eyes were beautiful bright like stars
Set over the bright red-bosomed morn,
His feet clutched round the frozen thorn,
And he pecked disdainfully at the bars
Of the branches round about, for he
Was there of will, for he was free,
And his song was merry and full of glee.

"I see," he sang, "the berries about—
Red hip and haw—and they are mine;
I hear the song and the laugh and shout
Of men who are near, and they think of me;
But the crow is sad on this leafless tree.
My lot is glad, but as for thine—
Go die, old crow, in the snow and frost;
If thou be dead, none will deem thee lost.
My branch sways up, and my branch sways down,
It would sway the freer if thou wert gone."

The crow sat sad on the leafless bough,
Thin though his feathers ruffled out,

His eyes were dim, and his voice was low,
Like a mariner's, dying upon the prow,
Who looks for land when land is none,
And sees life go with the sinking sun;
So the dying bird mourned sad and low,
Like the wail of winds as they wander slow
In the autumn woods; but I heard the song.

"The wind is chill and I am chill,
The wind is cruel and I am cold,
The frost hath bound the vale and hill,
And meadow and bottom have no loose mould.
The sun is dead, but he stareth yet
Like a dead man's eyes that are fixed and set,
And I shall be dead in some cold furrow
Before the night or the cold to-morrow."

The robin heard, but heeded not,
And flying away to a cottage near
Pecked at the pane till the children heard,
And opened the window to let him in,
For they loved the song of the Christmas bird.
So he slept that night in a warm dry spot
When the children hushed their merry din
Hearing the storm rave ere they slept

While the trees outside and their branches leapt
Like chainèd hounds beneath the whip
Or frozen rigging upon a ship,
And over the land the dry snow swept
Where the crow lay dead in a frozen furrow,
Nor dreamed of the thaw that would be on the morrow.

GROTESQUERIE.

Sitting in silence past all hope of change
   I entered the deep dreamland under thought,
And suddenly reality grew strange,
   Less living than the phantoms fancy brought.

For all my days were full of obvious things,
   My path was dust, and dust lay on the truth;
Caged like a bird, I could not spread my wings,
   And all my songs were such as fit not youth;

Till, in revolt, imagination fled
   From angry passions and their antidote,
The dull philosophy whose heavy head
   Mouths muttered wisdom that is got by rote,

And brought me long dark trains of consequent
   Conquest of vision realms, until my eyes
Fell on the strangest monsters ever rent
   From their old holdings. First I made my prize

Of hell's own imps, that various were and strange,
  Like bad dreams fretted into worse next night :
And culled, delighting quaintly to arrange
  A wild menagerie of dark delight,

From out of these some horned for a defence,
  And some fire-bellied, others terrible
With large device of fierce incongruence,
  And some with tongues like clappers of a bell.

And then I sought, despite fierce fang and claw,
  Shot forth and sheathless of the supple skin,
The white-toothed tiger, till he owned my law
  Even as the jaguar who had hushed his din

And trembled by the tawny lion's side,
  Who leapt and growled and cursed awhile and snarled
To purr at last; and going far and wide
  I caught up hideous crocodiles, hide-gnarled

And bitten fighting into loathsomeness;
  And serpents crowned and hooded, hollow fanged,

Plucking their poison bags to their distress,
   Coiling and knotting them; and these I hanged

About the beasts' big necks for amulets
   For their despite. Strange birds of dreadful plumes
And horrid clamour, caught in my wide nets
   I took, and those who dwelt in vampire glooms

With vultures' necks and bloody beaks well crooked:
   And then quaint things and beasts like ant-eaters,
With trunks and little eyes and sharp claws hooked,
   And garrulous beasts that up the scaly firs

Ran chattering, and all strange things indeed
   That are alive. Then I went further back
And plucked out skeletons, whereof the seed
   Is dead on earth, from death's capacious sack,

And made them live. The mammoth was of them,
   Whose tusks were curved like ship's bow timbers up
Over his head. He broke a large tree's stem
   Rubbing his hide thereon. His trunk the cup

Of a great rock hollow drained at one deep draught,
   So huge he was.   And then the mastodon,
At whom earth shook, and the large sky loud laughed
   To think that even this thing should be gone.

These I gave life, and me they followed while
   I sought the quainter, grimmer beasts whose bones
Lie crushed in earth beneath a heavy mile
   Of changed dead things that men call rocks and stones;

Like centipedes with jointed armour fine,
   There too the unimagined trilobites,
And wonders wreathed around in serpentine
   Long folds, like dreams of fearsomeness at nights.

And so I gained a wondrous following,
   But even so by no means was content,
But on my quest of quaintness wandering
   I found creations of old tales, back bent,

Distorted cronelike by the weight of age,
   With fabled features of long ancestry,

In the dark strata of a foxy page;
  And dragons flaming up old tapestry;

Dragons or griffins, brazen clawed, with scales,
  With fierce fire eyes and forked tongue's fiery breath,
And golden crooked beaks and scorpion tails,
  Whose barbed keen arrows surely sting to death;

And the chimæra, lion-headed he,
  The middle body of the nimble goat,
Tailed like the dragon; a strange mystery
  Of unknown meaning unto those who note

Real things with false. The terror too I gat,
  Rough-scaled and diabolical to sight,
Who on a mighty heap of treasure sat,
  Or roamed about the dreary hills at night,

A beaconed horror to the frightened folk,
  Who took their virgins to him by the score;
Though even then his plighted faith he broke:
  And then the double of the minotaur

I took and made him follow. Then, behold,
   I got me elfs and goblins, leprechauns,
Those living now, some from the age of gold ;
   Satyrs with hairy legs and peeping fauns,

And ghouls with pixies mingled were with me,
   A stonehenge brood with grave broods dancing round,
Veiled banshees wailing frantic prophecy,
   And wide-winged shrieking bats did there abound ;

While bright white moths danced at the beasts' bright eyes,
   And sharp teeth glittering that drawn lips disclosed,
Till muttered growlings suddenly would rise
   From dim black dens wherein strange things reposed.

These were my following, with many more,
   Sharp-finned sea-fishes swimming in the air,
Sword-fish and whales and orcs, that from each shore
   Came at my word, and did to me repair.

And the long beast they say lives not, yet is,
   The serpent of the sea, whose eyes are green,

Like shallow pools wherein weed tangle lies,
   And many shifting shadows can be seen.

It is the length of three great Vikings' ships,
   And underneath the hollow sea still grows,
With pulpy, shell-encrusted monstrous lips,
   That hide but half his hideous teeth in rows,

Sharp-pointed like the bitter coral reef;
   And on his dreadful head two horns there are.
With watchful eyes to aid his eyes in chief;
   And down his sinuous body many a bar

Of horrible colour glares; he has wide gills,
   Bloody to see and rough, and huge like gates
That keep the tide beyond the harbour sills;
   His tongue is triple-pointed, and he grates

His wormy jaws therewith to give him ease,
   Lying at rest upon the ancient slime;
While barnacles cling round, like leprosies
   About a man, that none shall shift by rime

Nor incantation. Thus the serpent sits,
   Lord of the horrible deep darks of the world,
Wound round in cable coilings over pits
   Wherein some lesser monsters might be curled,

Only he slew all others long ago;
   Since there were two a million years have passed;
Yet even he shall not for ever grow,
   And death, the charmer, shall charm him at last.

Even as I did, for the following
   Whereof I was the Comus for a while,
The monarch of a marvellous gathering,
   Who did upon his various subjects smile,

Saying: "These are my own, I set them round
   The palace I have made; in all the rooms,
In the dark places of the outer ground,
   In hollow corners, and in deepest glooms

I see my subjects. Ivory tooth and claw
   Stretched out or snarling, and again I see

Strange reptiles where but beasts I lately saw,
  And then imaginings of mystery,

And old delight of immemorial eld,
  And modern chattering apes and peacocks proud.
With elfins thereon riding who are spelled
  To an obedience. For all things are bowed

Unto my will, and come before my face
  (For I am weary of the things I know),
Making a quaintness of a common place
  Like barren ground where sudden puffballs grow;

For I have made a wonder of a spot
  Which was so bare, although the sightless scorn
Of dull blind men shall grope and see it not
  As I do now, and though the morrow morn

May take away my wild imaginings,
  And bring me to a duller, saner light,
Wherein this vaporous cloud of marvellous things
  Shall be an idle dream of yesternight."

DEATH AND THE PAINTER.

THERE is a painter (nay! let's say there was,
And so be merciful) who in his youth,
The beautiful youth that makes us gods, sinned once
And for that crime fell low. He was so young
And mightily visioned, like the prophets, and yet
Stumbled and fell. I do not say what sin.
Run ruin's records over; let it be
What thou abhorrest most, or what attracts
Thine undiscovered heart the most to crime,
And pity or condemn.

          He was condemned.
He who had been Isaiah's peer, or his
Who saw the complex vision of the wheels
And God's throne burning, or his who foretold
The last destruction of proud Nineveh,
Lay with the lepers, outcast and abhorred,
Impotent, chained, and driven. His slight hands
Laid down fair colour's sceptre, and he drew
No more for years.

And yet what thoughts were his!
What summoning suppliants of visions dear,
Never compelled to being, what ideals,
What passion, and what poesy and truth,
And what of Horror and immortal Fear!

. . . .

Lust drew a picture on his prison walls
Painted for darkness, as by phosphorus,
A very Janus figure, double faced
And double bodied, like two high reliefs
Welded together ; on the one side ran
Hair ruddy brown, as sunset seen on bronze,
Over fair shoulders on to breasts that knew
No infant's lips, and on the other side
Hair crisply curled, and short and fair, that decked
Bright brows of boyhood.   And Priapus laughed!

And afterwards came love, Urania,
And unseen drew her picture.   In one light
There shone a brightness.   Whoso looked thereon
Was dazzled, nevertheless, if he so held
His blind eyes to that spot, there came the sight
Of an immortal.   First two eyes shone out,
Two promises of God, and then two lips,
Fulfilment ; and a brow of prophecy.

It was the brow that spake, the lips were dumb,
For the Uranian knows but two great words,
God, Worship, and the light that haloes her,
Type of high silence, sings those two in flame.

And then came Death (and he of all the three
Alone put signature upon the walls
Under his picture), and behold! he drew
A dead man, and a serpent, and a sword,
And all upon a cloud that was as black
As hell itself, and a cloud was over them
Shining with unseen suns. And lo! the dead
Spoke, and as lightning runs from cloud to cloud
His soul went from the darkness to the light
And back again, the serpent watching it,
When suddenly God's angel sudden bright
Smote off the serpent's head, catching the sword,
And then the soul went upward. And Death drew
His veil aside, and he was beautiful;
Signing the picture—Life!

. . . . . .

And lo! the man
Cried with a terrible anguish: Lust is dead,
Love Dionæan and Uranian,
I am not worthy, worthy, even of death!

SONNETS.

OBSCURITY.

BLAME me not overmuch, if I must see
   Riddles in plain things ; or if things, close hid
   From thee, are open to me ; nor forbid
My comment thereon being obscure to thee:

Not being diviners, every mystery
   Has still an element some may not rid
   Their souls of, seeing that we live amid
The quick and dead of life's obscurity.

Could I know thee, yea, or myself, or speech,
   Whose thick breath chokes the spirit, I might fix
The very limits of hell, and heaven's reach,
   Which overlap upon this earth, and mix
Our souls, until at last each says to each :
    " Lo ! thy winged wisdom is an Apteryx ! "

LIFE.

REDWINGED Desire flew in a field of gold;
   From his white neck there hung a golden rood
   With the soft blood-light of sunned wings imbued,
Upon the cross piece there was graved "Behold!"
And underneath it there was faintly scrolled
   The legend, "I beheld"; below was strewed
   Straw without wheat, and, issuing thence, a brood
Of vipers, coiled around a worm in mould.

Looking thereon I said: "There is no ease;
   Link me, my sins, your bodies viperine,
   And choke me even as a twisting vine
Strangles a tree"; and as they rose to seize
   My dry throat, weary of the toil of breath,
   I saw Desire was struck by wingless Death.

NATURE.

She touched me softly as I sleeping lay,
   Silence and Speech she gave, who hath for name
   Darkness and Light, Terror and Love, the flame
Of suns and suns' eclipses, Night and Day;

Woman she is, and yet unborn, I say,
   And spirit ; yet maternal raptures claim
   Her veins and bosom ; she is queen of shame,
Virgin as Venus fresh from foam and spray.

Whom she desires must die, but shall arise,
   For, being unruled, she is omnipotent :
Fulfilling, faith-filled, her own prophecies,
   She is like God, self-worshipped, and is bent
By her own altar, and upon her lies
   The atonement for herself, prayer-penitent.

CREDO.

What do I care for all the clash of creeds
   And rabid reasonings of vanity,
   Whose roar and rush go round and under me
With passions worse than lust for empire breeds?
For that which most contemn fulfils my needs,
   What they desire I would not care to be,
   So to my god I shout my Evoë,
And pipe upon my simple pipe of reeds.

My holiest holy is to them profane,
   And therein they with cursèd feet would tread
     Only my god shows greater than their own;
     For he is free from blood, and he alone
   Hath the still halo shining o'er his head
Of promise like the rainbow in the rain.

THYSELF AND THINE.

This be thy task. If thou hast aught in thee,
   Faint not with fear nor any touch of shame,
   For as thy words are so shall be thy name,
Eternal, and thy soul's epitome.
They are not as the foam-script of the sea,
   Feeble and passing frail as bodiless flame;
   But more enduring than thyself, whose claim,
Though large for love, owns its mortality.

Thy work is twice thyself: it has thy sight,
   And the far circles where the spirit soars;
The little worn path of the eremite.
   And the wide ways wherein the sunlight pours;
The sacred foam on ocean's neophyte,
   And all the waters held by all his shores.

SIN AND THE MAN.

Gird up thy loins and get thee from this place,
   The damnable city of thy dark soul's plain,
   For fire shall burn the couch where thou hast lain,
And slay the woman with the lustful face.
Take up thy staff and scrip, for by God's grace
   There is a respite from the awful rain;
   What thou hast cast away He gives again,
Saving one soiled pearl, thee of all thy race.

She shall be smitten, not with leprosy,
   To make her lovely body like her soul;
   But with an endless flame wherein to moan;
And she shall shriek for ever unto thee,
   Calling thee bridegroom, until God shall roll
   The earth to hell's mouth for a seal and stone.

THE POET'S MANSION.

This is my house; and therefore do I dwell
   In what no hands have made nor shall unmake;
   It could not tremble though the heavens quake.
My soul has built it, and I love it well;
And therefrom, like the spirit in a shell,
   I sing my songs for art and nature's sake,
   Sending forth music, soft as any flake
Of light fallen down from bright spheres tunable.

Some, therein deaf and doubtful of the alms
   I give, pass by me half in scorn and shame;
   But those whose hearts are like the stars to tame,
Whose spirits are self-crowned with deathless palms.
Whose passions are seas zoned with storms and calms,
   Catch fire and song from me like flame from flame.

AFTER YOUTH.

How changed Love is, how weak and wan, alas!
   Where are the odours now his locks once shed?
   Grey has he grown, and for his crownèd head
His rosy wreaths are garlandings of grass;
His smile is not so precious as it was,
   Nor is he now that passionate god who led
   My hungry soul to her who rose and fled,
Veiled in a heavenly way I could not pass.

Ah, let her go! I never touched her soul,
   And all my pictured pleasure was as vain
     As love's great words when he was bright of hair;
Ah, let me go, grey god; I ask no goal
   Of high Elysium on your lowly plain,
     If only peace may smile upon me there.

LOVE AND THE LAW.

BE not cast down, but rather be glorified
  By the exceeding passion whose dread growth
  Shadows our lives; and, answering for both,
I speak with bated breath my awful pride
At our mixed destiny; for side by side
  Love sets us, and though murder slew my strength,
  And my death killed you, we shall lift at length
The heads we bow when in his realms we bide.

While such as we come to his throne above,
  Though there were one strong god who could make
    pause
  Death on his steadfast way—not even he
Could dare define Love's kingdom unto love,
  Or mock the resolution of Love's laws,
    Or break Love's power to break captivity.

LAUNCELOT TO GUINIVERE.

TRADITION, honour, custom, and the schools
  Stand in our opposition rank on rank;
  Our strongest forts are but a piercéd bank,
And though we mend we toil with broken tools:

And yet I care not: though I were of fools
  The very love-fool, though my mention stank
  On every puffed-out breath, what draughts I drank
I still would swallow from life's bitterest pools.

Yea, look, my queen, while those deflowered lips
  Hunger for mine on this desirous mouth,
    I will scorn honour and pluck it vauntingly
From duty's garland that is dead and drips
  With blood of useless battles whose hot drouth
    Yields as I yield and drink and drowse with thee.

ON A PICTURE.

A LITTLE gold of sunshine clasps the land,
   That is so chafed and worn perpetually
   By driven winds and the old toiling sea,
Whose scant brown harvest gleams upon the strand;
And on the height the wannest ruin stands,
   Storm wasted, wherein dwell but shadowy
   Ghosts of dead hearts and moon-waned memory
Like dead flowers in a beautiful dead hand.

Pour from thy heart, O sea, oblation sweet,
   And fling foam garlands on their wind-worn tomb,
The hollow earth whereunder all things meet;
   And for a space, O sky, arrest thy doom
Of shade and rain, for surely our sad feet
   Shall not avoid at last the death-wind's gloom.

TO EMILIA.

Ah, do not blame my heavy idleness,
   For in these hours the seed-field is of rhyme ;
   The rainy spring is not my fruitful time,
Stay but awhile and in the autumn bless.

Behold the meadows—and our souls not less
   Than space wherein we walk and lift sublime
   Our heads that touch the stars—and own our clime
Hath its soul-seasons like the earth we press.

No hour is lost—no moment—in the dusk
   Of dawn or night-time or the open day—
     Or any dream-hour gone from memory ;
Each thought grows darkly till it breaks the husk,
   The leaves foretell the fruit, and when I say
     These words their seed-time was my speech with thee.

LOVE AND APOLLO.

I wind no horn that comes from Fairyland,
   I touch no Merman's lute or Triton's shell,
   Not mine the pride of Marsyas who fell,
I yield the gods their own with knee and hand;
If aught I sing be pleasing or withstand
   Chill chiding winds, like the blue flower's bell
   On Alpine heights, I own the miracle
Of great Apollo's smile and Love's command.

Sweet are their gifts! O merman of the sea
   Watching thy maiden with her golden comb
Coil the cold tresses that entangle thee,
   And thou, strange foam-child of the fertile foam,
Ancient of azure waters; and, ye fays,
Blithe be your songs, I sing mine own these days.

www.ingramcontent.com/pod-product-compliance
Lightning Source LLC
Chambersburg PA
CBHW032246080426
42735CB00008B/1030